Have a

Fantastic

Marriage

Happiness For
Forever!

by Gail Cassidy

Disclaimer and Terms of Use:

The Author and Publisher has strived to be as accurate and complete as possible in the creation of this book, notwithstanding the fact that he does not warrant or represent at any time that the contents within are accurate due to the rapidly changing nature of the Internet. While all attempts have been made to verify information provided in this publication, the Author and Publisher assume no responsibility for errors, omissions, or contrary interpretation of the subject matter herein. Any perceived slights of specific persons, peoples, or organizations are unintentional.

Printed in the United States of America, First Printing,

Tomlyn Publications
547 Shackamaxon Drive
Westfield, NJ 07090

http://www.coachability.com

Have a

Fantastic

Marriage

Happiness For
Forever!

Table of Contents

MARRIAGE TIPS

Marriage has its ups and down, but remember one very important fact: Our perspective and our state of mind create our reality. To give you a silly, but apt example, "To her lover, a beautiful woman is a delight; to a monk, she's a distraction; to a mosquito, a good meal." Everything in life depends on how you look at it. When in doubt, step into your spouse's shoes.

Remember Tip #1, See the invisible tattoo on your spouse's forehead that reads: **"PLEASE MAKE ME FEEL IMPORTANT."**

Enjoy reading the Top Ten Lists and the Tips. Highlight those you want to keep in the forefront of your mind. Enjoy every day of your life. Each one holds a surprise for you. Look for it and when you find it, write it down, keep it forever.

SUGGESTIONS from Hallmark:

EACH MORNING
greet the dawn with joy. Look into one another's eyes with the bright possibility that shines with every rising sun. Offer one another encouragement in your endeavors and support for all you'll encounter

throughout your day. Send each other out into the world with a kiss and a smile.

EACH DAY
nurture one another's talents and individuality. Respect each other's work, applaud each other's efforts. Hold sacred your time together, as well as your need for solitude. Share the chores and the challenges, the serious and the silly. And watch for the magic of unexpected pleasures, the comfort of easy laughter.

EACH NIGHT
talk of the big and little things that made up your day. Put any differences to sleep before you turn out the lights. Relish the quiet--be tender, be playful, be passionate. Savor the sweetness of each kiss, the softness of each touch. Fall asleep in the shelter of one another's arms.

EACH YEAR
be one another's truest friend so that your joys may be doubled and your sorrows halved. Be flexible with what life brings you--never be afraid to reassess your dreams. Celebrate your special days and achievements, for they are mileposts on your journey together.

ABOVE ALL, remember to honor and nourish the beautiful love that first connected you, one to the other.

**Wishing you both a FOREVER
filled with love and happiness!!!!**

MARRIAGE SUGGESTIONS

1. See the invisible tattoo on everyone's forehead that reads: **"PLEASE MAKE ME FEEL IMPORTANT."**

2. Find at least one happening in each day to be grateful for.

3. Look for positives in your spouse.

4. Recognize the specialness of your differences.

5. Provide an atmosphere conducive to happiness, e.g. pictures, lighting, comfort, simplicity, etc.

6. Vary your daily activities. Do something different that will revitalize your marriage.

7. Remember, humans of any age need breaks.

8. Know that everyone you meet has something special to offer.

9. Living in the moment is where you find happiness.

10. Learn the Serenity Prayer: "God, grant me the serenity to accept the things I cannot change, courage to change the things I can and the wisdom to know the difference."

11. "See" and/or "feel" your positive day before you climb out of bed. Use positive self-talk.

12. Be (or act) enthusiastic about everything you do. It's contagious; it carries over to the people in your life.

13. Accept your spouse as he/she is, and then provide the atmosphere for them be happy and grow.

14. Learn from your spouse.

15. Ask yourself, "Does it really matter?"

16. Being right does not always work, e.g., Here lies the body of William Jay, who died maintaining his right of way. He was right, dead right as he sped along, but he's just as dead as if he were wrong.

17.   HAVE FUN!

ATTITUDE

18.   Park your ego at the door; it hinders relationships with your family.

19.   Give your family a reason to check their negative attitudes at the door also.

20.   Know that your spouse "mirrors" you. They reflect what they see, hear, and feel from you.

21.   Shake things up. Make changes. "If you always do what you have always done, you'll always get what you've always got."

22.   Show your special other through your own example what fun having a great attitude is.

23.   Be patient.

24.   Positive attitudes are catching wherever you are.

25.   Show respect to get respect.

26. Know that attitude is a choice everyone makes every day.

27. Remember, you cannot help what happens to you, but you are always in charge of your responses.

28. Remember, there is a pause between stimulus and response. Choose your response carefully.

29. Ask yourself why you are choosing to be unhappy, bored, tired, sad, happy.

30. Know that attitude is the steering mechanism of the brain. Body language can lead to attitude.

31. Practice changing your attitude by sitting or standing straight, with your head up and a smile on your face. It does work!

32. Know that it is the attitude of our hearts and minds that shape who we are, how we live, and how we treat others.

33. Help your family recognize their specialness.

34. Success is feeling good about yourself every single day. That is attitude.

35. Know and share with your family that true power is knowing that you can control your attitude at all times.

HUMAN RELATIONS

36.   Treat your spouse as if he or she is the most special person in the world.

37.   Never talk down to your spouse.

38.   Find what is really special about your special someone.

39.   **SMILE.** It warms a room.

40.   Use tact when responding to an upset spouse. The rewards outweigh "being right."

41.   Know that sharing your negativity doesn't work. Your state of mind is your choice.

42.   Be 100% fair at all times--no exceptions.

43.   Keep in mind that perception is reality--yours and your friends and family's.

44.   Treat your love as you wish to be treated.

45. Understand that no one wants to be wrong.

46. Everyone desperately wants to feel special.

47. Remember that people gravitate toward things that are pleasurable and avoid things that are painful. Make learning pleasurable.

48. **LISTENING** is the greatest compliment.

49. Try to understand before being understood.

50. Show genuine appreciation to your spouse for the little things s/he does.

51. Begin corrective action with sincere and honest recognition of what has been done correctly.

52. Never embarrass him/her. Allow the person to save face.

53. Use encouragement. Make the error seem easy to correct.

54. Don't be afraid to admit your mistakes. It will make you appear more human.

55. Show respect for every person's opinion.

56. Challenge your spouse to be the best that they can be.

57. Make **SINCERITY** your No. 1 priority.

COMMUNICATION

58.   Set standards in your everyday life and share them with your family.

59.   Know the purpose and importance of what you are doing.

60.   Set high expectations.

61.   Know that 55% of all messages comes from the body. Notice how you can tell your special someone is in a bad mood without any words being spoken.

62.   Know that 38% of the message comes from the voice: inflection, intonation, pitch, speed, e.g., "I didn't say he stole the exam." Seven words-- seven meanings.

63.   Know, you cannot **NOT** communicate.

64.   Recognize that we don't all see the same thing when looking at the same thing.

65. Know also that we don't all hear the same things even when listening to the same words.

66. Control your thoughts; your feelings come from your thoughts; therefore, you can also control your feelings! Choice is control.

67. Take responsibility for what you say and how you say it.

68. Listen for the message, yet know that body language can be interpreted as only a clue to the meaning of the message, e.g., arms crossed in front of chest could mean blocking you or it could mean person is actually cold or comfortable.

69. Learn to lead rather than to try and overcome resistance.

70. Communicate your enthusiasm through your body and voice.

71. "One who is too insistent on his own views, find few to agree with him." -Lao-Tze

72. Speak with a warm heart.

SELF ESTEEM

73. Know that a person with high self-esteem does not need to find fault with others.

74. Remember that people find fault with others when they feel threatened, consciously or unconsciously.

75. Know that self-esteem is not noisy conceit. It is a quiet sense of self-respect, a feeling of self-worth. Conceit is whitewash to cover low self-esteem.

76. Remember, people, even spouses, have two basic needs: to know they are lovable and worthwhile.

77. Remember, it is a person's feeling about being respected or not respected that affects how s/he will behave and perform.

78. Helping your spouse build his/her self concept is key to being a successful partner.

79. Know that your words have power to affect your spouse's self-esteem.

80. Each person values himself to the degree s/he has been valued.

81. Words are less important in their affect on self-esteem than the judgments that accompany them.

82. The attitude of others towards a person's capacities is more important than his possession of particular traits.

83. Bragging people are asking for positive reflections.

84. Masks are worn to hide the "worthless me."

85. Low self-esteem is tied to impossible demands on the self.

86. Your own self-acceptance frees you to focus on others, unencumbered by inner needs.

87. The single most important ingredient in a nurturing relationship is honesty.

88. Ask this: "If I were to treat my friends as I treat my spouse, how many friends would I have left?"

89. Avoid mixed messages. Be clear in your statements of expectations.

BOUNDARIES

90. Tolerate no disrespect.

91. Be consistent.

92. Set boundaries.

93. Find opportunities for each other to improve the quality of his/her work.

94. Differentiate between the action and the person.

95. Uncover and address, when possible, the reasons for conflict within your marriage.

96. Make sure you understand his/her perspective.

97. Focus, as often as possible, on what is right rather than what is wrong.

98. Give plenty of recognition for the unique gifts of each other.

99. Keep in mind that you have power in the present moment to change your thoughts, feelings, and attitude about the past.

100. Take control of your life by focusing on the present.

101. Remove the word "try" from your vocabulary. "Try" to pick up a pencil. Either you do or you don't.

102. Find the lesson or value in unacceptable situations.

103. Know that you have choices in spite of your past experiences.

104. Turn problems into a learning opportunity.

105. Have a clear vision of where your marriage is going.

106. Approach problematic situations with relaxed confidence.

107. Respond thoughtfully to challenging and/or problem situations.

108. Avoid making judgments.

109. Learn problem solving:
                State the problem
                Look for causes of the problem
                Brainstorm solutions
                Choose the best one

110. Always see beyond your own point of view.

111. Encourage habits of thought conducive to growth in understanding each other, to think outside the box.

112. Recognize that there is no one interpretation of a situation.

LIFE'S TREASURE TIPS

113. Begin to be now what you will be hereafter. - St. Jerome. Repetition is the mother of skill.

114. Know that you too are special.

115. Enjoy each day and each moment of life.

116. Make corrections by citing two positives for every negative.

117. Live in the present.

118. Be alert for moments of gratitude.

119. Show lively enthusiasm!

120. Create an atmosphere of fun.

121. Build on successes.

122. Create a routine with varied activities.

123. Know you are made for one another.

124. Visualize doing well.

125. Be relaxed.

126. Make each other feel important.

127. Remember, "You are what you choose today." -Dyer.

128. Give yourself opportunities to succeed.

129. Provide a safe atmosphere.

130. Validate each other frequently.

131. Your reality is what you make it to be.

132. Polish your people skills.

133. Hone your communications skills.

134. Take excellent care of yourself.

MORE TIPS

135. Work towards feeling good about yourself. It is a person's highest goal and feeling good is contagious.

136. Always do what you feel is right or true.

137. Your actions reveal your values.

138. Your thought is the most powerful force in your universe. "Nothing is either good or bad but thinking makes it so." -Shakespeare.

139. Whatever you dwell on expands.

140. Work toward goals that cause you to feel a sense of mastery.

141. Write a list of everything you have accomplished or have been recognized for in your life. Add to it whenever you think of something new. Read it when the going gets tough.

142. Have a clear sense of purpose in your marriage.

143. Clarify your goals and focus on them

144. Be a risk taker. Step outside your comfort zone. Try something new.

145. Positive expectations are the single, most outwardly identifiable, characteristics all successful marriages possess.

146. You can train yourself to think more positively by training yourself to choose what you pay attention to and what you say about it, both to yourself and others. "We know what we are but know not what we may be." -Shakespeare.

147. Whatever you believe, picture in your mind, and think about most of the time, you eventually will bring into reality.

148. Your self-image is the most dominant factor that affects everything you attempt to do.

149. Nothing is more exciting than the realization that you can accomplish anything you really want that is consistent with your unique mix of natural talents and abilities.

150. Remember, "Change your thoughts and you change your world." -Norman Vincent Peale.

WORTHY QUOTES

- Assume a virtue, if you have it not. - Shakespeare.

- Act enthusiastic and you'll be enthusiastic. - Carnegie.

- It is not the place, nor the condition, but the mind alone that can make any one happy or miserable. - L Estrange.

- Beliefs have the power to create and the power to destroy. -Robbins.

- Nothing is more likely to help a person overcome or endure troubles than the consciousness of having a task in life. -Frankl.

- When the student is ready, the teacher will appear. - Zen proverb.

- The ancestor to every action is a thought. - Emerson.

- Imagination is more important than knowledge. -Albert Einstein.

- Things do not change; we change. -Thoreau.

- Great men are those who see that thoughts rule the world. -Emerson.

- Nothing has any power over me other than that which I give it through my conscious thoughts. -Anthony Robbins.

- The greatest discovery of my generation is that human beings can alter their lives by altering their attitudes of mind. -William James.

- The only limits you have are the limits you believe. -Wayne Dyer.

- Anything we fail to reinforce will eventually dissipate. -Robbins.

- Patience is the companion of wisdom. -Augustine.

- The more he gives to others, the more he possesses of his own. -Lao-Tze.

- Vision is the art of seeing things invisible. - Swift.

- Believing is seeing. -Dyer.

- What makes a happy marriage? It is a question which all men and women ask one another.... The answer is to be found, I think, in the mutual discovery, by two who marry, of the deepest need of the other's personality, and the satisfaction of that need. - Pearl S. Buck [Originally submitted by Charles Powell, who can be reached at cpowell@pacifier.com.]

- Seldom or never does a marriage develop into an individual relationship smoothly without crisis. There is no birth of consciousness without pain.
  - C. J. Jung
  [Submitted by Charles Powell, B.S. Ed., Coach, who can be reached at cpowell@pacifier.com.]

What the mind can conceive and believe, it can achieve. -Hill

The Top 10 Quick Financial Tips for Newlyweds

Beginning your life together is a happy and exciting time. It is also a good time to begin laying the groundwork for a strong financial foundation.

1. Begin looking for reliable financial experts.

Ask family, friends and co-workers to recommend a competent advisor. Interview several before agreeing on one. You and your spouse should both feel comfortable with the expert you choose.

2. Set goals.

Whether it's a house, starting a family or regular contributions to a mutual fund, these goals will secure your future. Discuss them with your advisor and make sure you and your spouse agree on them. Keep in mind, this may mean a compromise!

3. Immediately begin planning for retirement.

It's never too early to plan for retirement. Meet with your employer to discuss 401k plans or retirement funds available. If possible, contribute the maximum allowed by the plan.

4. Examine your insurance needs.

Life insurance through your employer is usually enough until you have children or buy a house. Your death will be devastating to your spouse. You certainly don't want to burden him/her further by leaving financial stress. Each time you have a child or purchase a new home, meet with your advisor to adjust your policy.

5. Make a will.

It's hard to accept that there may be a need, but accidents and illnesses do occur. A will protects the surviving spouse.

6. Pay off loans and other debts ASAP.

The more quickly you can pay off "old" debts, the more quickly you and your spouse can begin fulfilling your financial dreams and goals. Get rid of this "baggage."

7. Begin saving now.

Even if only in small amounts. You've heard it before, "pay yourself first." Having a financial safety net is important to the health of your marriage.

8. Begin investing now.

It's the habit of regular investing that grows wealth. Establish fiscal ground now for your new household.

9. Create a budget.

Even a loose budget is better than no budget at all. You and your spouse should develop a budget you can agree on and support each other in sticking to it. Remember to include regular "splurges" such as an occasional night out to keep the romance alive.

10. Keep things in perspective.

Remember, to some, money is symbolic of something else - control, comfort, power... Take time to discuss financial issues with your spouse before they become a problem.

[Originally submitted by Laura Terrebonne, Personal/Professional Coach, who can be reached at dltbone@usit.net.]

The Top 10 Rules for the Game of Life

We have all been given our precious life. How can you take yours to the next level of happiness? Start by realizing the following:

1. Life is NOT a Game.

There is no dress rehearsal.

2. This is YOUR life.

This is not somebody else's life. Do what you really want to do. Learn to put yourself first.

3. You no longer have to live by shoulda's, coulda's, oughta's or if only's.

Live in the present and make each day perfect for you. Have no preoccupations with your past or future. Don't let others' beliefs that don't work for you determine how you will live your life.

4. There is no such thing as TRYing.

Simply put, there is really no trying--either you do it or you don't. Put your arms down in front of you; now try to lift your arm. Did you do it? My point is that either you lifted you arm or you didn't. Trying is not full effort and doesn't portray your commitment.

5. Success is what YOU define it to be.

If you believe you are successful, you are. Success is measured in numerous ways. If you are intrinsically successful then it would be very difficult not to let

6. YOU are perfect just the way YOU are.

Stop focusing on your shortcomings. Start loving yourself and your uniqueness and special gifts.

7. Listen to YOUR inner wisdom.

It is this voice or intuition that helps guide you and your decisions.

8. There are many lessons to be learned.

There is a lesson to be learned in every triumph as well as every failure. Look for the lessons.

9. You need to have a vision.

Having a vision is the first step toward having the life you want. Purpose gives meaning to your life and changes your attitude and perspective about life.

10. YOU must take actions.

If you want a more satisfying, fulfilling and balanced life, you must begin taking actions to create it. Status quo is not good enough when you have a gap between where you are and where you want to be. Set goals to support your vision and your dreams. Focus on results and if you're not getting the results you want, find the reason.
[Originally submitted by Natalie A. Gahrmann, M.A., Coach U Graduate, and author, who can be reached at nataliegahrmann@hotmail.com]

The Top 10 Principles to Achieving a Life Beyond Balance

Recognition that words like balance or juggling don't fit is finally here! Switching off at work about what is happening at home and putting life into pockets is meaningless. It requires sacrifice or conflict. The beautiful integrated, flowing, harmonious way that people wish to live is beyond this. This Top Ten gives tips for achieving a fulfilled and guilt free life, without sacrificing the people or things you love.

1. Design the life you want.

It seems obvious, but it is easier to say what you don't want. Make a clear statement to yourself about the life you want. Be specific. Every day take one step towards achieving that dream - focus on what is possible, not what is impossible. Say no to what you don't want.

2. Know what your values are.

Think of a time when you felt honored, fulfilled, and happy and describe this to yourself or a friend. Listen to how your values show up and from today do nothing that would dishonor these. Ask - what is the cost to me of not honoring my values?

3. Live your life fully in the moment.

Be present in every moment, conversation and relationship you have. Know that when you forget this, you lose so much time and energy it is catastrophic. You can waste a day wondering what to do next, instead of enjoying what you are doing. Watch your children - they are experts.

4. Value your dream time.

Spend moments just wandering in your head or physically visit the place you dream you will live in or hang out. Gather pictures of what this future will be like. Behave like the person you want to be. Make your dreams real. Now.

5. Know what your limits are.

Putting up with things about yourself, the way people treat you, your environment, and your possessions uses up energy that would be better spent else where. Set these limits selfishly!

6. Chose how you will be.

I am self-conscious, untalented, unworthy, too busy......No! Say, "Until now I have chosen to be self-conscious, untalented., unworthy, too busy, and from today I chose to be confident, talented, worthy, and live my life at the pace I love"

7. Know what might stop you.

Identify the things that you know might stop you and be ready for them. Identify what you might do to sabotage this process and who might get in your way. Prepare, notice and react positively.

8. Have a support network.

Someone who supports you in your dreams and aspirations and is there for you when you need a friendly face is essential for this to work. A coach, a partner or a friend will keep you on track and encourage you when things get tough.

9. Make now the right time to start.

Listen to yourself say - "This will work when I have more money/time/space/when the kids have grown up.......Give it up! Phrase the things you desire in the here and now

10. Start now.

Have a handful of things that you do every day that are just for you - a good cappuccino, a hot bath, time with your children. This will nurture you and remind you of the commitment you have made to having a beautiful integrated, flowing, harmonious, wonderful, fulfilled life that is YOURS!!

[Originally submitted by Mairi Watson, Founder partner of Professional Life Coaching, Life Coach, who can be reached at mairi@professionallifecoaching.com)

The Top 10 Rules for Creating a Better Life

It's said that it's the simple things in life that truly give our lives meaning. Here are 10 tips for creating that better life:

1. Count your blessings daily.

Even with life's challenges, there are always positive things, people, and events in our lives that keep us going. Make a list of those things in your life that keep you fueled, and give thanks for them daily.

2. Do more than you are getting paid to do.

Going the extra mile brings many unexpected rewards into our life. Remind yourself that it's a privilege to be able to add value to someone else's life.

3. Shake off your blunders.

Whenever you get knocked down by life, don't look back on it too long. Mistakes are life's greatest teachers; they help us grow and move on to higher planes, but only if we remain unstuck.

4. Reward yourself in the best way you can after a period of long labor and achievement.

Stretch your reward by sharing it with someone special.

5. Remember that you are God's perfect creation; you can do anything you dream of anytime you want.

6. Let your actions always speak of your values.

Be on guard for false pride and deceit that may halt your progress.

7. Every day should be unwrapped as a precious gift.

Life may offer hurdles and stumbling blocks; use these as stepping stones to reaching your goal.

8. Live this day as if it were your last.

Today is all you have. Run with it!

9. Extend everyone you meet all the care, kindness, love, and understanding you can muster, without thought of reward.

Give of yourself: your time, your money, your talent or skills. Take the focus off yourself. Your life will never be the same.

10. Laugh at yourself and at life.

Laughing causes a release of tension and worry, and clears your mind to think clearly toward a solution that is certain to come as soon as you let go.

[Originally submitted by Carmen Stine, Personal Development & Media Coach, who can be reached at coachmentor@aol.com.]

HAVE A GREAT MARRIAGE!